Pickup Artist in an Hour

How to Get a Girlfriend this Weekend

Jonathan Green

Copyright © 2015 Jonathan Green

Simultaneously published in United States of America, the UK, India, Germany, France, Italy, Canada, Japan, Spain, and Brazil.

All right reserved. No part of this book may be reproduced in any form of by any other electronic or mechanical means – except in the case of brief quotations embodies in articles or reviews –without written permission from its author.

Pickup Artist in an Hour has provided the most accurate information possible. Many of the techniques used in this book are from personal experiences. The author shall not be held liable for any damages resulting from use of this book.

ISBN: 1512339806
ISBN-13: 978-1512339802

FREE GIFT

Thank you for your purchase of my Pickup Lines kindle book, as an extra bonus I want to give you a free gift. This is a copy of my ORIGINAL pickup artist guide. I sold this for $37 and it has ten times more of my top secret dating techniques. If you want to go beyond the pickup lines and connect with beautiful women then you need this guide.

==>> http://servenomaster.com/dating

CONTENTS

	Acknowledgments	i
1	Before You Leave the House	1
2	Arriving at the Venue	3
3	Starting the Conversation	5
4	Becoming the Guy She is Talking To	8
5	Maker Her Attracted to You	10
6	Find Her Passion	13
7	The Power of Truth	17
8	Don't Compliment Like a Jerk	19
9	Keep Your Goal in Mind	21
10	The Girlfriend Path	22
11	You Must Touch Her	24
12	Use Your Eyes	27
13	The Seduction Path	29
14	Enjoy the Journey	30
15	Final Words	32

INTRODUCTION

Hello guys and welcome to Pick Up Artist in an Hour. In the hour it takes you to read this, I'm going to give you all the information you need so you can go out and start meeting women tonight.

I've been meeting and connecting with stunning women for nearly a decade now. I started out just like you. I was terrible with women and I had no idea what to do.

Most of us grow up with this idea that we are either good with women or terrible.

Nobody ever told me that I could get better.

The day I found out It was possible to get better with women I became unstoppable.

With that one piece of knowledge and the tools in this book, you can be meeting stunning women TONIGHT.

You can easily get a new girlfriend by next week.

I have dated models, actresses, Olympic athletes and pretty much every type of beautiful woman you can think of.

I have had threesomes and every other crazy adventure you could ever desire in the bedroom.

I want you to be able to have exactly the same epic experiences.

I'm going to give you a couple of the tools that I use, with my in-person students. I have tested these with phone and live students over and over again. You can get out there and just get those first conversations going. None of the content in this book is based on theory, opinions or concepts.

It is all 100% based on science and experimental rigor. Everything in here has been tested over and over again by me and many of my coaching students.

Your goal tonight could be really simple, it could just be going out and just talking to one girl, even if it feels like that's not a big goal, remember that every little step leads to more successes and that's kind of how I want you to view this entire process.

Don't compare yourself to anyone else. Don't compare yourself to me, or anything like that. I just want you to compare yourself to yesterday. If you did a little bit each day, in a year you would be 365 steps closer to your goal and believe me that's more than enough steps to completely change your life.

1 BEFORE YOU LEAVE THE HOUSE

The first thing you want to do is pick a venue where you are going to go, just pick a club where you know there's going to be a goodly amount of girls that you are attracted to and there's kind of a good vibe.

In some of my advanced lessons, I talk about club architecture but the main thing is you want to find a place where you can be heard. If you are not good at dancing, find a place where there's a large non-dancing area and you want to find a place just where there are lots of girls and the vibe is not a sitting vibe.

You want a vibe where everybody is just standing around the bar, standing around the area just moving around a little. That type of movement is very conducive to meeting girls. It makes it a lot easier.

Walking up to a table where everybody knows each other is a little bit more challenging. It's totally doable but right now we want to start with something easy and fun. Why make it hard when you can make it simple? That's really my philosophy.

You can do this work in a bar or cafe or house party. It really works anywhere. I really like to meet women at night with a cocktail in my hand so I'm a big fan of bars and clubs.

Just pick somewhere that has a lot of opportunity. A lot of different women you can talk to.

So I want you to put on an outfit that makes you feel cool. I have 3 levels of how I dress. My most casual is wearing a cool t-shirt and jeans and yet I've been very successful with this. I find that in different areas, dressing differently leads to more success.

In Tennessee I have done a lot better dressed casually, than I have when I go out wearing a really cool tie, so you just never know about formality. But just wear an outfit that makes you feel cool. How you feel is way more important than anything else so just put on an outfit that makes you feel good about yourself.

The easiest way to master fashion is to look at what all the men in the venue are wearing. Then just dress 10% better than them.

If all of the men are wearing polo shirts, then wear a button down shirt and a skinny tie.

You want to stand out by being one notch better dressed than the competition. That's all it takes to win in the fashion game.

If you really aren't sure how to dress well, my buddy has a great video teaching fashion at ServeNoMaster.com/fashion.

When you feel kind of comfortable and head out, maybe you're by yourself, maybe you have a wingman, a buddy to go out with you, either way, you just want to head out to the bar and kind of have a little bit of a plan.

You don't need to overthink. You just want to choose a place where it's natural to talk to women and you want to wear clothes that make you feel cool and confident.

2 ARRIVING AT THE VENUE

Now tonight I don't want you to drink, I don't want you to get your courage or confidence from alcohol, I want you to realize confidence can come from within.

I've tried searching and meeting women in every environment without drinking just to prove I can do it. I didn't drink for 90 days last year and I didn't drink for most of the first six months where I learned how to meet women. It's really important that you don't become dependent on alcohol for confidence or the ability to be social.

That is a crutch that will eventually fail you and only cause you more problems in the end.

It's okay to have one or two drinks but I often find that one or two drinks turns into five or ten for a lot of guys so tonight just have water, maybe have juice, or just have a coke. It doesn't matter, but I find that having a drink in your hand makes everything a bit more casual. Just make sure it's not alcohol.

I want you to go to the bar and just kind of catch the vibe. During the first drink you don't have to do anything. The first drink is your time to just be relaxed and be casual. I never talk to women during my first drink at the bar, as that's kind of my special time and I want you to feel the same way.

You don't have any obligation during that time, it's time to catch the vibe, kind of get casual and know that there's nothing you have to do. You can just get peaceful and be really comfortable and kind of scope the vibe.

My favorite place to talk to women is in the line at the bar because it's so easy. Everything I do is tactical and as soon as you make your life one of situations, meeting women becomes easy.

I always, always, always get in line behind women when I want to order a drink. I go out with guy after guy who is like "I never meet women in bars" and they always go and line up behind other guys. Well you have already taken away an easy situation so the first thing you should do is when you go for a drink, whether its your first drink or second drink, make sure you line up behind some girls!

These tiny little steps. Each one gives you a little more opportunity. I am always making opportunities for myself. It's why I'm so successful with women.

Pay attention to when women are near you. When there is opportunity. If there is a short line with 2 guys at the bar and a long line where you'll be stuck behind 20 women, I want you to take that longer line. Make meeting women a priority. Just be willing to create situations that make starting conversations easy.

3 STARTING THE CONVERSATION

There are a couple of things you can do to start a conversation with girls and just keep it really simple. It doesn't have to be complicated.

So what I want you to do is just be like "excuse me are you girls in line?" Just asking neutral questions like these starts a conversation.

I've met and dated hundreds of women through this one simple sentence. It's my most common opening line because it doesn't express any interest. It doesn't give anything away. It's just something you say to guys and girls.

You are just trying to find out the situation with lines like "excuse me are you guys in line?" or if it's a group, "excuse me, are you guys all ordering together or is one person ordering for everyone?"

You can even try "I love waiting in line but I don't want to wait forever" and any kind of follow up where it's just casual. It's okay if the first time your heart's racing and you are really nervous. That's okay. I've been through all those phases and over the course of the next weeks that's all going to go away. The main thing for you to do is just to say something just to get used to talking to girls.

If you make your purpose about saying something. Just trying to say something to a woman to see what happens. Then this process can be really easy.

What makes talking to women, especially attractive women, so hard is that we have intent. It's like if you're talking to a woman because you want her. Well that's intent. You have this motive. But if you remove her from the equation. If you are just talking to her to practice and see what happens. That's a lot more fun. You remove the stress element. So make it a game.

Just go out tonight and say the lines above and see if I'm telling the truth. Make it about me. Instead of you. Be like, "I'm going out tonight to see if that Jonathan dude is full of crap. I'm going to try these lines and see if he's a liar. And if they don't work I'm refunding this book."

That's ok. I can take it. I know the lines work and I know that mindset will make it easier for you.

Now maybe you are a little bit more advanced. You have talked to a few women. You've had a lot of girlfriends. Or maybe you are a beginner. It doesn't matter. Either way, just go in and this is a great way to start conversations. Talk to a couple of girls at the bar each time you go up for a coke, water, or whatever. Each time you start a little bit of a conversation. That's a great way to just kick-start yourself because you are not risking anything.

Now the second thing that I want you to do is a little bit more of an advanced opener, a little bit more of an advanced way to start a conversation.

Just walk up to a group of girls. I want you to use what's called an opinion opener where you kind of get their opinion and be like "excuse me girls, if you thought your boyfriend was cheating, would you check his phone, would you check the texts in his phone?"

Girls love talking about this topic. They love talking about relationships and they love talking about the unknown, things like the spiritual world, palm readers, etc.

But for now we are going to stick with relationships because it's easy. The reason this is so powerful is because you find out which girls have boyfriends, which girls have a trusting nature and which girls aren't really trusting and that's kind of what we are looking for. We are really trying to get to know people and build a connection that way.

Everything I believe in is about building a fast powerful connection and really meeting the real person. With this conversation starter you will immediately find out how they feel, you really can have that kind of chat.

This is so powerful because it ALWAYS starts a great conversation. And we say it in a way that's a little bit nervous because that's charming. You can say this one line to a group of girls and they might talk about it for thirty minutes or an hour. You just get a lot of practice having a conversation with a group of beautiful women.

4 BECOMING THE GUY SHE IS TALKING TO

The second thing you want to do is to change the subject. In different dating systems this technique has different names - transition, change, alternate, or move forward. You just want to go from the guy who just walked up and said something to the guy that they are talking to.

Think of this as changing into someone who is three dimensional. If you only talk about one topic, then you are a one-topic person. Even if you talk to her for thirty minutes, as soon as her friends walk up she will disappear. Because she doesn't feel any connection to you. For a woman to feel a connection you must discuss at least two totally different topics. That's how you become real to her.

Whether you are talking to two girls that you just met in the bar line. Whether you are talking to a group of girls. You want to move the conversation forward. The easiest way to do that is to make an observation and you can keep it really simple.

Just point out something you like about them like "I love the way you guys seem so comfortable with each other" or "I love you that guys seem like best friends, that's so cool, have you guys been friends for ten years?" or "I love that necklace, it's just so cool" and "you know a lot of people don't take their time with fashion, that looks cool."

You are just making observations to move forward and it's about keeping it simple. As we go more advanced we can do a lot more technical things here. You just want to kind of change the subject from that first topic to a separate topic. Then you want to go to "how do you guys know each other?"

This is a great thing to say because it kind of gets the vibe of "oh have you guys been friends for a long time? You guys look really close, did you guys just meet?" And immediately people love to tell you their story.

Girls that have known each other for ten years will talk about how they met in kindergarten. Or maybe that's twelve years ago not ten. Or they will talk about "oh we just met a year ago" and you are like "wow, you guys seem so close!" You are just kind of interacting with them. It doesn't have to be big. It can just be simple. You just walk up and say "hey are you guys in line?....hey are you guy's best friends? You guys have such a cool vibe together" and then maybe they will ask you about your best friend and you can respond and talk about that.

Now these are the opening movements okay? And tonight it's okay if your goal is to just get through these two opening movements. Do this five or ten times a night and you will be amazing in a month!

This is exactly how I started and exactly how a lot of other guys started. It's a great path for a beginner. I want to take you through the entire progression. If you are really brave you can go all the way to kissing a girl tonight, getting a girls number, taking her home, whatever your goal is its all doable tonight with this basic introductory system.

This is really designed to be something that you can learn and succeed with in a single night. Just focus on each step until you master it. Then try the next step.

5 MAKE HER ATTRACTED TO YOU

So now you have chatted to her for two or three minutes. You want her to become attracted to you. There are three things women are attracted to: self-confidence, passion and honesty.

These are the three pillars of my entire system. It's that simple. A lot of times we think, "oh it has to be really complicated! There are hundreds of things women are attracted to - I have to be tall, I have to get rich, etc." Those things don't matter for right now.

I've dated women way richer than me, way taller than me, and way better looking than me. Right now you might be thinking about me – this guy is super ugly or you might be thinking he is so handsome. I've heard them both from different people. People have different opinions about me. But those opinions don't matter at all. It's about how I feel about myself and that's all you need to understand.

It comes from within. You can either be somebody who has attractive qualities or you are a person who is attractive and the core elements of attractiveness are again – self-confidence, passion and honesty.

Self-confidence it the hardest thing to really just have so what I want to teach you is the idea of "fake it till you make it." This idea is that you will act like a self-confident person here while you build up how you actually feel about yourself.

Eventually, the way you should feel is that you are the coolest, best looking, most amazing guy in the club and I want you to have the feeling that when a girl walks away from you she just made a terrible decision.

That should always be your mindset, be like "wow I can't believe she walked away from me." That self-confidence is exactly how I am able to punch above my weight. It's all about believing in yourself.

When a girl rejects me I just think that she missed the chance of a lifetime. It's like she judged me too quickly and made a terrible decision. She voted without getting all the information. And now for the rest of her life I will always be that one great thing that she missed out on.

It doesn't hurt my self confidence when a woman rejects me. Because I see it the other way around. The only possible reason a woman could reject me is because she didn't have all the facts. Or she is a terrible decision maker.

That's how you should feel as well. She's not rejecting you. She's rejecting your approach. Which you can improve. It's not your core personality. She hasn't had a chance to see that yet.

So what can you do to build instant self-confidence? What I'm going to teach you right now is the short cut. What I want you to think is "I'm going to give this girl fifteen minutes to make me think she is cool, and if I don't really feel that she is cool in fifteen minutes I'm going to walk away."

This mindset is pretty much unstoppable. It reverses all the terrible thoughts that normally get trapped in our heads. Most guys approach a woman and are thinking about how to impress her. That's weak. So she is on a pedestal and he is on his knees begging for a chance with her. I don't respect guys like that. A lot of dating systems teach that mindset. I steal girls from them. My students steal girls from them all the time.

Because our mindset is so much stronger. Just walk up and see if you guys have a connection. If she doesn't impress you in the first fifteen minutes, just move on. I move on all the time. There are tons of women who aren't a good fit for me. So why waste her time or my time?

This will remove ALL the pressure you are feeling when you talk to a woman. This on tiny tweak. It will shoot your confidence through the roof. Even if you are faking it. And super nervous inside. You will LOOK really confident.

Now these exercises are very powerful.

Here is something that you can try during a regular day. Just try this with anyone you talk to throughout the day. The checkout girl at the grocery store. The guy who pumps your gas. Anyone.

Talk to three people and imagine that each of them has one million dollars and if they like you enough they will give it to you. Then I want you to talk to three more people and imagine that you have the million and if you like them enough, you will give it to them.

As soon as you change your mindset, your body language and your micro-expressions and how you interact will completely change. Your confidence and body language change based on how you feel about yourself.

When you imagine having the money. You will be so confident. Instead of trying to make the person like you. You have reversed everything. Now they have to do all the work. And it's so great. This is all in your head and it can change your results with people.

It's exactly the same thing with our 15 minutes technique. If you have ever talked to a girl you don't think is attractive but then your buddy thinks she is really beautiful and he starts acting weird, objectively she hasn't changed. The only thing that's changed is how he feels inside. All it is, is within of you.

99% of the battle of getting a beautiful girlfriend, getting in a relationship or getting you know that connection, whatever you are looking for with women is within yourself and as soon as you realize that, you are ahead of 90% of other guys walking around on the planet.

Most guys think that women have all the power. They don't realize it's within. So what I want you to do is when you are talking to this girl, I want you to find a reason to stay, instead of looking for a reason to walk away or waiting for her to reject you, that's not the mindset I want you to have. I want you to realize that you are in control and you have the power.

Just let her be the one to show how great she is. This will make talking to women a LOT easier for you. You will seem confident which is the first of our three pillars of attraction.

6 FIND HER PASSION

Now when I meet women, I try to think of them as like a mine, a coal mine and I believe there is a diamond in there. I think everybody has something that they love about themselves and I try to dig for that and through the conversation, one of the ways I dig for that, is that I say, "what do you do? not like what's your job? But what do you love to do."

When you ask people this question you find out who the real person there is and you start building a real connection. That is a very intense question and she is going to ask you to answer the same questions. She'll go "well what do you love about yourself?"

That's great because answering that question demonstrates confidence, believing in yourself, knowing who you are and the answer itself doesn't matter. It doesn't matter if your favorite thing is painting war hammer 40,000 figures, it doesn't matter if your favorite thing is reading dungeons and dragon books or going to Star Trek conventions, if that it's your thing.

It's your sales pitch and when I teach you about pitching later on, I'll show you that you can talk about video games or anything as long as you talk about it without shame and with confidence, the woman will be attracted to it.

I've talked to women about comic books that I love; I've talked to women about going to comic conventions. I love wearing costumes. I talk about all these things in a way that shows that I'm confident and passionate about them and that's how we kind of transition from self-confidence into passion.

Passion is knowing what you love to do. There are a couple of things that I really love to do. I love traveling, I love dating, I love teaching guys about pickup and I love teaching about dating, whatever you want to call this. I tell a lot of women that this is what I do for a living. I say that I am a dating coach because I love talking about it.

It's something I'm passionate about and immediately it's interesting because I feel good about it. I don't feel like its creepy or sleazy, I'm not shy about it. My face is everywhere on my websites and I have no problem with what I do. I love talking about it because it's my passion. I really want to make nice guys win!

I'm tired of all the jerks getting all the girls. I want nice guys like you to get the beautiful women and breed out all the jerks that picked on guys like you and me in high school. Maybe you were awesome in high school; maybe it was just me that was on the debate team.

But as you are talking about passion, and you can see how I just feel so excited when I talk about it in my videos, that's how you should talk about what you love.

I learned about passion from a girl that I dated. There was a girl that I hooked up with a couple of years ago and it was amazing. I was really into her for three or four months and it took a lot of work. She was one of the first girls I got with when I was learning to be a pickup artist.

I always thought she was dumb in the back of my mind. I thought she was really hot but dumb. We were talking in the morning after a night together and she started talking about how her dream was to become a masseuse and she was like "I just want to go to massage school. I want save up enough money working in bars to go to massage school so that I can help people. I just want to make people feel a little more relaxed after a hard day at work."

She was so excited about that, even though she was stunning and we had already been intimate together, in that moment she was so attractive to me and even now, over three years later, that's the moment I remember from us. Not the night together and not the craziness.

I still remember that but the moment that sticks out is the moment where she opened up about her passion.

I would never want to be a masseuse. I think it seems like a lot of work

- it makes your back hurt; you have to touch a bunch of gross people… Objectively I don't like the profession. I don't get massages because they make me feel uncomfortable.

Even with my objective opinions, her passion about it changed the way I felt and that's the same thing you can do when you talk about what you love and when she talks about what she loves and the idea is to get past the regular boring questions.

Everyone asks about work and I've met women from pretty much every profession, everything from lawyers to doctors to janitors to glass collectors in bars and there are a lot of people that love talking about their work but guess what, it's pretty much always boring for me.

I don't want to hear about something I've heard a thousand times before.

I met a stripper at a really, really expensive club in London whose passion was painting and she knew that she needed thirty paintings to have a gallery showing and so she tried to talk about stripping and I go "that's not interesting" and we immediately had a conversation that she doesn't have with other people and that's kind of man you want to be. We talked about her paintings and it was something different for both of us. Of course she gave me her number after a chat like that.

You want to be the exception. You want to be different from other guys. And you want to have different conversations.

So now that you expressed your self-confidence and talked about something that you are passionate about, I will give you a second question that is really powerful.

The second question besides what do you love to do is "if you could go anywhere tomorrow morning, where would you go?" Now girls who are often testing me will often go "is it a vacation or am I moving?" That doesn't matter. You want to push past it and go "just imagine I am a genie and I can snap my fingers and you are somewhere else in the world, where would you go?" The first answer is not going to matter unless it's terrible.

One time a girl answered somewhere that there was a train ride away; like a thirty-minute train ride. I was like "5 dollars, you can go easily. I can grant a wish and that's what you want, you are so limited."

But many girls will give you amazing answers when you ask "why?" This follow up question gives you the real information that you are looking for. I had a girl when I was in Europe and she talked about an island that I had never heard of in the Caribbean and I was like oh she wants to lie on the beach all day but when I asked why she started talking about how her grandmother lived there. She had never met her grandmother but she really wanted to connect with her.

So it's the second question that is important when it comes to getting to the heart of the matter. You are looking for that diamond.

This is the phase where you are building that attraction, building that connection, showing that you are something different and also finding out what makes her special. Your goal is to find out something amazing about every woman you meet.

I have walked up to and talked to probably thirty to fifty thousand women in bars over the last three or four years. That's a lot of women. I don't remember their names, I don't remember what they look like but I try to remember the amazing things and the most amazing stories are what I'm telling you now.

Those are what I recall, years and years later. So find out what makes her special.

So now you know how to do two of our three pillars. You can show self confidence with our simple 15-minute trick and you can do passion just by asking her these 2 powerful questions.

7 THE POWER OF TRUTH

Let's talk about honesty. Honesty is a complicated subject. The first thing you need to know is that everyone in bars is lying, whether women are lying about their age or men are lying about their income, people are putting up a fake front.

This is reason I can get a girl even when competing with a ton of guys. I know that if I go into a bar and there is one beautiful woman, even if there are five hundred guys in there, I can compete with any of them because I know who I am and I'm comfortable expressing that and that's kind of what you want to move towards.

It takes a long time to become at one with yourself and to develop all these advanced feelings but the main idea is that you are comfortable telling the truth.

Think about when you lie. You lie to your boss, pretending to be sick when you are just going out partying. You lie to your parents when you were in high school and you snuck out or you got drunk or whatever you did and got into trouble. And you lied to your girlfriend when you don't want her to break up with you.

In each of these scenarios you lie to people that have power over you. As soon as you lie to a girl in a bar, you are telling her "I have to lie to you to make you like me." That means she has the power. You are creating this relationship and I don't want you to have that feeling.

There is no one who is better than you.

I am really comfortable with myself. I love myself and I get tons of women. I have all these great things going on, but that doesn't make me better than you. It makes me different than you but you should always feel like this when you meet me. We are equals.

This is the only place where relationship can exist, even where friendship can exist. So as you are talking to this girl, by being honest you are saying you are equals. And even when two equals meet they can still have to prove that they should still be friends because there are millions of equals out there.

So by being honest and being yourself and this is exactly what this passion stuff is about, you are talking about what you really love to do. You know a lot of people lie about their jobs or lie about other aspects of their life you know?

I never lie to women.

I'm not good at remembering my lies, so there's no point in even trying. Sometimes I used to tell a joke or two like something that wasn't really true and then I forget which girl I said it to and I created a whole problem. It's not worth it.

It's funny a little bit but it keeps you from getting any girls and really that's the goal, it's to get a girlfriend, get a relationship, get a kiss, get a number, get laid. What I want you to do is be really honest and this is really where complimenting comes into the picture.

8 DON'T COMPLIMENT LIKE A JERK

A lot of people don't understand how to compliment. If you have read anyone else's material on dating or you have seen any of the stuff out there and there are thousands of websites out there that I know of, then you know that they always say don't compliment women.

What those people don't understand is that it is not the compliment itself; it's how you deliver it. If you say to a girl "wow, you are so beautiful" a lot of times you are waiting for her to say something back.

You are waiting for her to say thank you. You are waiting for her to give you her number. You are waiting for her to say that she really likes you. By asking for her to give something back, you are giving away your power. You are giving away the value of the statement.

Think about this: if you walk into like an art gallery and you look at the Mona Lisa and you go "wow, that's a really great painting." The painter is dead. He is not going to hear you. Yes I do know its Leonardo da Vinci code. But what I want you to understand is that you have to compliment from a place of – "I'm a guy who says what I want and I don't care if you react." So you say that you like the painting not because you want a reaction or a reply. You say it because it is something inside of you.

I was in Hawaii for all of November for my thirtieth birthday and it was awesome and I was out with a guy, a buddy who was trying to learn some of this stuff and I wanted to show him how powerful compliments could be.

So I walked up to a girl who was really, really pretty and I go "excuse me, I know you're with your friend, but your outfit looks amazing. You know a lot of people come to Hawaii and they just wear flip-flops and shorts. You are wearing a really pretty dress and it looks amazing" and then I walked away.

That made the compliment so powerful because I didn't need anything back and that's kind of the position I want you to work towards with honesty. When you tell a girl she is pretty, you say it not because you need her to react or get her to do anything. You don't have to care if she says thank you, what you have to do is express your emotions.

I don't ever want to die at the end of the day with an emotion left over that I should have released. I really believe in releasing positive energy into the universe, however you want to call it. I just want to put the goodness within me out into the world and so if I think a girl looks nice I can say that as long as I am saying it from a position of I am one with myself.

I know who I am, I'm solid, I'm really comfortable with myself. You know I've seen guys walk up and say the most astounding things to women. One of my friends walked up to a girl on the streets of London and said "excuse me your breasts are amazing."

You think that's inappropriate? You can't say that to a woman? But he just believed it so much he just had to say it. And of course the conversation went well because he felt that was okay. Because he is really expressing his true inner self.

Right now we are just kind of kick starting, I just want you to go out tonight and have a really good time and kind of realize how you can build conversations but these three elements, self confidence, passion and honesty, they are the tripod on which you can build a powerful relationship and you can build these connections in less than ten minutes.

You don't have to spend an hour and a half talking about your childhood to build a connection with women and that's what I kind of want you to realize for tonight.

9 KEEP YOUR GOAL IN MIND

At this point in the conversation you have built a little bit of a connection, you've built a little bit of the chat and found a little bit about each other, you have a little bit of an attraction. At this point, if she is still talking to you, she is interested!

If a woman is still standing there talking to you in a bar it's because she is still interested. When women get bored, they walk away.

I've seen it thousands of times. I've seen it in a friendly way and I've seen it in a brutal way. If she is still talking to you, she is a bit interested.

You know there are 34 signs of attraction?

You can look for hair touching, you can look for eye dilation; there are all these subconscious things but all you want to look for is - has she walked away. If she is still there, you are still in the game!

So now you have to think about your destination, and there are two directions you can go in. You can go in the "I want something to happen tonight" direction or the "I want to go on a date direction." And they are two different directions.

One is about building a sexual energy and one is about building a relationship energy and you know yourself better than me. I'll tell you the truth, when I meet different girls, I'll react. I'm all about reacting the moment. Sometimes I'm really in a sexual mood and I'll go in that direction but sometimes I just feel like she is a perfect girlfriend and I'll go into that direction.

10 THE GIRLFRIEND PATH

So if you want to go into the girlfriend direction, which is awesome, you want to build what is called comfort. Comfort or rapport is when you are facing each other and not-rapport is when you are facing in two different directions.

You really want to build that connection to where the universe revolves around the two of you. Now if that's the case, what I want you to do is play something called the question game.

This game has two rules, just go "you know what? You are so cool, lets play a game, the game only has two rules, rule number 1 you cannot repeat the other person's question, rule number two, you ask the first question."

Now what's amazing is that 90% of women always say to me, "No you have to ask the first question" even though that means she has to reveal something first. Now this conversation is very powerful.

You can go in a sexual direction with it but you can also go in a comfort direction, a connection direction, just be like "what makes you happy?" or "What kind of food do you like to eat?"

This is where you can ask those questions, but what I want you to do is listen to the questions she asks you. Her questions are more important than her answers. You might say to her, "have you ever been in love?" It's a great question, you are kind of going in that boyfriend question direction.

This is kind of where it is okay to do that a little bit and she might say "have you ever had a threesome?" Well guess what!?! She is on the sexual path and you have to make a decision, you can either try and drag her over here or you can go with her, and that's the same thing, as you are asking questions, you might want to ping her sexually, be like "have you ever kissed a girl?" and if she goes "no, what's your favorite color?" well now you know she has kind of put a wall there.

So you can think of this conversation as becoming a river because you ask a question, then she asks a question. Her questions will reveal what direction she wants to go in and this is where you can feel the connection.

11 YOU MUST TOUCH HER

Now while all this is going on, the second thing we need to talk about for the whole conversation is touch. I'm only going to give you the basics now. There are a lot of words for touch. Some people call it kino (short for kinesthetic) but I call it Skinship, which I learned in Japan.

Skinship is the idea that if you are friends with someone and you don't touch, it doesn't exist, it's like a dream.

When I first came to Japan I was teaching in a high school and I saw guys lying on each other, pulling each other's hair and I was like "wow, I guess those are the gay kids" but they weren't. Those guys were the toughest guys with the most girlfriends.

They are so comfortable with their sexuality in Japan that they always assume someone is not gay whereas here we always assume someone might be gay. We lean towards the other direction and so men don't touch other men for fear of seeming homosexual and men don't touch other women for fear of seeming creepy.

So what I want you to do is realize that touch is a form of communication, if you take a baby and you give it food, milk, nourishment, light, a blanket, a warm place to live and no human touch, the baby will die within a few weeks.

I read a bunch of scientific studies on this, it's called gentle human touch. The idea is touch is important. Touch is what keeps us alive and it's how we can communicate. Touch is how I can meet girls who don't speak English and it's not a problem.

So now that we understand touch is important, you want to be a guy who just touches. Over the course of the next week, I really recommend you start hugging all your guy friends, shaking hands with your guy friends, increasing the touch.

All the guys I know who are the best with women kiss each other on the cheeks when they see each other and I didn't see one of my friends once for three months and when he saw me he kissed me on the cheek and he was crying a little bit because he missed me so badly. It's okay to be an emotional guy. Guess what? Those guys get the most girls. I'm telling you it's okay to be that way.

So let's talk about touch in the most basic sense, I want you to think of it as three zones. If you get to zone two, you own zone one. If you get to zone three, you control all the zones and also the face is part of zone 3. So while you are talking to the girl you want to physically escalate, you want to move forward physically. You want to build up your Skinship.

If you talk to her all night and don't touch her, and she becomes attracted, she'll start thinking – why is he not touching me? We don't want that to happen so what I want you to do is start off working the arm and what you want to do is an accidental touch. In each zone, think accident and then on purpose. Two types of touch for each zone.

So you just tap the side of her arm by accident with the side of your arm. If you are sitting down side by side you can touch the side of your legs to each other. Just make it seem accidental, then when you are talking to her just a quick touch and let go. Just a light touch and release and that's kind of how you take the territory.

What you don't want to do is this - you don't want it to be slow and you don't want to watch it and you don't want to hold on so its really about not looking, quick touch and let go and what you are doing is getting her used to you touching her. You are slowly building it up. Think of boiling a frog. If you throw a frog into boiling water it jumps out, but if you put a frog into water and slowly boil it, it will not jump out, and that's the same thing with touch and Skinship.

So just be a person who touches, if you feel creepy, she will feel that you are creepy. You have to feel comfortable with your touching, so you touch the back of her arm you're like wow that's so cool and you let go.

Then what I love to do is do an arm around the shoulder and release and be like "wow everybody in this club is so crazy tonight" and then release. Then you touch her arm a little bit up higher.

You are just working up accidentally on purpose, getting her used to you touching. As you build the touch along, you want your touch to match your conversation. If you are having a sexual conversation the touch will of course turn sexual, and if you are having a romantic conversation you might want sort of hand holding.

This avoids that awkwardness of going for a first kiss or something and that's your first touch. That's the biggest mistake guys make with girls on first dates. They wait too long to touch her. It's a form of communication and it's really important to women.

So what you want to do is have your touch go through the three zones along with your conversation. Start out in zone one when you first meet. Shake her hand. Accidentally touch her arm.

Then as you are getting into building attraction you can start doing zone two. Touch her shoulders. Just put your arm around her for like 2 seconds. Look around the room and make a general comment. "Everyone in here wishes they were having a conversation as good as we are."

Then zone three is where you go for the kiss. She's ready because she is used to touching you. You are familiar to her.

12 USE YOUR EYES

So now while you are doing all your verbal progression you're also doing your touch progression. These are the three overarching pillars. The three forms of communication are words, touch and number three is eye contact.

Eye contact is so powerful. I've seen guys get girls with nothing other than eyes. This is one of the most powerful techniques I've seen. If you are taller than a girl especially, you can just start coming in like a snake and she will be drawn in like a tractor beam.

I've done this to guys in a lot of demonstrations and I'll show you some pictures and videos if you take the free gift from the front of the book. In the actual touch sections of my membership site I have videos of me taking advantage of guys and controlling them with my eyes but its so powerful.

Most people do a triangle. If you think about when you are talking to a woman, you look in a triangle around her face – from eye to eye to mouth and back around again. Or you do the center of the forehead, side, side, and back to the center of the forehead. That's kind of how I look. Everyone does a triangle. Our eyes are always moving around like this.

If you just keep steady eye contact and stare in her eyes, the blinking doesn't matter. But if you keep staring into her eyes, you build an amazing sexual tension, and an amazing sense of attraction.

They did a huge study on people that do speed dating, and I'm sure you've heard of speed dating. When you go there, you get a three minute date with like thirty people, what they did is they took two groups of speed daters.

The first group for the first thirty seconds wasn't allowed to talk but they had to stare into each other's eyes then they talked for two and a half minutes. The second group talked for three minutes. The first group had way more matches. Everyone in the first group was rated as more attractive than everyone in the second group.

Staring and eye contact is really powerful and you just kind of want to just do it a little bit more than you normally do. If you normally look away every five seconds, look away every six. Just build yourself up to be someone who just looks into someone's eyes. There's something about it, it's powerful, it's magnetic, it's like a tractor beam.

So over the course of the conversation, how long you look at her eyes will become longer and longer and longer and then when you feel that moment for kissing you do that head tilt that we all do when we kiss and you just have it. It's the only reason we ever tilt our heads.

To build that sexual tension with eye contact just stare into her eyes and count to five. You probably won't make it past three. That's how powerful this technique is. But as you do it. Both of you will become more and more attracted to each other.

This is as far as I'm going to take you in your first night. I think if you work on all these elements it's going to go really well.

You know what?

I'm going to take you all the way.

Let's cross the finish line.

13 THE SEDUCTION PATH

I will teach you the first way I ever got a kiss using techniques. It's a great classic and it's really simple. You are talking to a girl and you go, as soon as you think to yourself "should I kiss her," this is the time to ask this question because she is already there, "you look like you want to kiss me."

There are only three possible answers she can give you – yes, no and maybe. The first time I ever asked a girl this question she screamed, "are you f@%king with me?!?" right in front of my face, in front of hundreds of my friends at a big party.

My interpretation was - that's a no. Just so you know, we did sleep together that night. So even the worst answer falls into a category, yes, no, or maybe. If she says yes, please kiss her; please kiss her immediately!

If she says maybe, say "let's find out" and lean in. If she says no go "oh sorry, you looked like you just looked like you were thinking of something" and that's exactly what I said to that girl.

20 minutes later we were making out in an alley and 90 minutes later we were back at my apartment. So don't think of it as a wall, it's just another path. So if she says no, just go "oh sorry, you looked like you were thinking of something" and move the conversation forward.

That's the best and the easiest way to get a kiss out of a girl. Now if you want her number just ask for her number. At this phase, at the end of the conversation, if you wanted to take her home, just be like "hey you know what? Lets get out of here".

14 ENJOY THE JOURNEY

I don't want to make it complicated right now. There's a lot more advanced and complicated techniques that I'm going to teach you later down the road but go for that kiss tonight, go for that number tonight, take a girl home with you, whichever one you want to do and realize it's the first step of the path.

Just having some amazing conversations is okay. Otherwise I have given you a ton of information that is swirling around in your head and that's okay. I want you to have some ideas but the main thing I want you to do is to have fun.

I love meeting women, I love talking to women in bars, I love taking guys out and meeting women with guys, I love partying, I love meeting and having adventures. It's why I take so many pictures and why I have traveled around the world.

I do what I love and I want you to have that same feeling, I don't want it to feel like a chore, just think - this is so much fun, this is so cool, women. As soon as you get past that first fear barrier that you are going to get rejected you will see that there are amazing, beautiful women that have the most amazing and kindest stories.

The coolest girl I know in the whole world is a formula one model and a Corona model from Austria. She is literally the coolest girl I know and she is stunning. If you have this idea before you get into this stuff thinking that the more beautiful a woman is, the meaner she is going to be, it's not true.

This is a journey and I want you to go out tonight thinking I'm going to meet amazing people. People are cool, in general. People that go out are cool. They are friendly and they are looking to talk to people. People don't go out looking to talk to no one. If women didn't want guys to talk to them, they would get all dressed up and then they would sit in the kitchen.

So with that final thought, I really want you to go out tonight.

15 FINAL WORDS

There is a comment section at the bottom of my Amazon page and after you go out tonight just leave some comments about adventures you have had tonight or anything you think I can add to this book.

I'm always looking to improve my lessons, I'm always looking to communicate with you guys, Write about your experiences tonight, what went right, what went wrong and we are just going to keep moving forward, this is just the beginning because I promise you, your life is going to be different, I know what I'm doing and I'm very good at what I am doing and it is very important to me that your life becomes better, I'm very excited for you guys, thank you for becoming part of my family.

If you have gotten this far then I'm really proud of you. Head over to ServeNoMaster.com/dating and grab your awesome free gift.

I hope your dating dreams come true.

Jonathan Green
aka
The Inimitable LondonPaladin

ABOUT THE AUTHOR

Jonathan Green is a world traveling master pickup artist who has taught students around the world. He has seduced models, Olympic athletes and famous musicians. He has lived in over a dozen countries and currently lives with his much younger girlfriend on a tropical island. He surfs, kayaks and makes love every day. He marches to the beat of his own drum and live his life with but one promise. He will serve no master.

Website

http//ServeNoMaster.com

MORE FROM THIS AUTHOR

If you liked this book on being a **Pickup Artist**, also checkout my **Pickup Lines** book as well. This book has ten of the best conversation starters in the world. They work in every situation. You never have to run out of things to say again!

Click here for more details on my **Pickup Lines** book:

http://ServeNoMaster.com/lines

Printed in Great Britain
by Amazon